MY FIRST LOOK AT COMMUNITIES

MANY SUBURBS ARE QUIET, LIKE SMALL TOWNS

A Suburb

VALERIE BODDEN

CREATIVE EDUCATION

Published by Creative Education

P.O. Box 227, Mankato, Minnesota 56002

Creative Education is an imprint of The Creative Company

Designed by Rita Marshall

Photographs by Getty Images (Photographer's Choice, Photonica, Stone, Taxi, The

Image Bank)

Copyright © 2008 Creative Education

Printed in the United States of America

Library of Congress Cataloging-in-Publication Data

Bodden, Valerie. A suburb / by Valerie Bodden.

p. cm. — (My first look at: communities)

Includes index.

ISBN-13: 978-1-58341-514-6

1. Suburbs—Juvenile literature. 2. Suburban life—Juvenile literature. I. Title.

HT351.B62 2007   307.74—dc22   2006019355

First edition 9 8 7 6 5 4 3 2 1

A Suburb

Outside the City

A suburb is a place just outside of a city. Most suburbs are smaller than cities. They do not usually have any **skyscrapers**.

But suburbs do have lots of houses. They have stores, too. There are offices and schools in suburbs. In most suburbs, the houses are in one area. The stores and other buildings are in another area.

HOUSES ARE THE MAIN BUILDINGS IN SUBURBS

Most suburbs are much quieter than cities. But there is still a lot going on in suburbs. Cars drive through the streets. Kids play on playgrounds. Some people shop at stores or go to movie theaters. Others grill hamburgers in their backyards.

LIVING IN A SUBURB

There are suburbs all around the world. Lots of people live in suburbs. Most of them live in houses. In some suburbs, most of the houses look the same.

About half of the people

in the United States

live in suburbs.

MANY HOUSES IN SUBURBS LOOK THE SAME

SOME SUBURBAN HOUSES ARE HUGE AND HIDDEN

In other suburbs, the houses all look different. Most houses in suburbs have big yards.

Many people who live in suburbs work in the city. Most of them drive their cars to work. Some **carpool**. Others take buses or trains.

Some people work in suburbs, though. They might work in offices or stores. Some people are police officers. Some deliver the mail. Kids in suburbs go to school.

Driving cars from
suburbs to cities can
make a lot of **pollution**.

SUBURBAN ANIMALS

Lots of animals live in suburbs. Most of the animals are pets. They live with people. Some people in suburbs keep cats or dogs as pets. Other people keep birds or fish.

Other animals that live in suburbs are **wild**. Deer are wild animals. Sometimes they go into suburbs. Rabbits and squirrels are wild animals, too. Lots of rabbits and squirrels live in suburbs.

The kids' movie *Over the Hedge* is about animals living near a suburb.

SUBURBAN YARDS HAVE ROOM FOR PETS TO PLAY

You can find all kinds of birds in suburbs. Robins and cardinals are birds that live in some suburbs. Other birds called crows and woodpeckers live in some suburbs, too.

LOTS OF ROBINS LIVE IN MANY SUBURBS

Suburban Fun

Suburbs have lots of fun things to do. Most suburbs have stores to shop at. Many suburbs have lots of restaurants to eat at, too.

Some suburbs have parks for kids to play in. Some have swimming pools. You can take long walks through suburbs. You can bike through suburbs, too.

New York City and the

cities around it have

more than 500 suburbs!

SUBURBAN PARKS ARE GOOD PLACES TO PLAY

Lots of people who live in suburbs go to the city to have fun. They can go to the city's zoo. They can visit the city's **museums**. Or they can watch a play. Then, they can leave the busy city. They can go back to their house in the quiet suburbs!

SUBURBAN FAMILIES CAN ENJOY QUIET NIGHTS AT HOME

Hands-on: Make a Suburb

Suburbs are fun places. You can make your own suburb to explore.

What You Need

A piece of poster board

Magazines

Scissors

Glue

Markers

What You Do

1. Look through the magazines to find pictures of houses and other buildings. Have a grown-up help you cut out the pictures.
2. Glue the pictures onto the poster board. Put the houses in one area. Put the other buildings in a different area.
3. Draw roads between the buildings.
4. Draw some people in your suburb. Draw animals, too.
5. Imagine what everyone in the suburb is doing!

IN SOME SUBURBS, THE HOUSES ARE CLOSE TOGETHER

Index

Words to Know

carpool—when people drive together in one car

museums—places where paintings and other important things are kept and shown

pollution—something that makes the air, ground, or water dirty

skyscrapers—very tall buildings that look like they can touch the sky

wild—an animal that is not a pet

Read More

Pancella, Peggy. *Suburb*. Chicago: Heinemann Library, 2006.

Schlepp, Tammy. *My Home*. Brookfield, Conn.: Copper Beech Books, 2001.

Trumbauer, Lisa. *Living in a Suburb*. Mankato, Minn.: Capstone Press, 2005.

Explore the Web

Ben's Guide: Your Neighborhood http://bensguide.gpo.gov/k-2/neighborhood/index.html

Field Trip http://www.hud.gov/kids/field1.html

National Geographic: The New Suburb? http://www.nationalgeographic.com/earthpulse/sprawl/index_flash-feature.html